MAKING DECISIONS

MAKING DECISIONS

MAKING THE BEST DECISIONS OF YOUR LIFE

MICHAEL JAMES FITZGERALD

OVERDUE BOOKS PUBLISHING

Third edition, January 2014 (rev. 20210604)

E-book edition:

ISBN-10: 1-887309-29-2

ISBN-13: 978-1-887309-29-5

Print edition:

ISBN-10:1-887309-27-6

ISBN-13:978-1-887309-27-1

Overdue Books Publishing
http://www.overduebooks.com

CONTENTS

Introduction   vii
What Is Your Decision about?   xiii

1. Brainstorming Your List   1
   Brainstorming List   5
2. Your Top Ten   7
   Top Ten List   9
3. Your Top Five   11
   Top Five List   13
4. Your Top Three   15
   Top Three List   17
5. Number One   19
   Your Number One   21
6. Take Time to Process   23
7. Your Decision   25
   Your Decision as a Sentence   27
8. Concluding Thoughts   29

About the Author   31
Also by Michael James Fitzgerald   33

INTRODUCTION

Over 30 years ago I was faced with a really tough decision. I was a young man, recently married, and about to become a father for the first time. I'd been attending junior college but was spinning my educational wheels. I'd been in school for two years but hadn't picked a major that I felt completely right about.

I'd picked several majors—including one that I loved—but I knew that if I took a job in the industry of that major, I'd be on the road most weekends. It wouldn't be a family-friendly career. The major fit *me* well, but not my lifestyle. It was time to face reality and change direction.

The Reflection Method

Most of the decisions we make are small and seem to have little impact on us, but some decisions have a lifetime impact.

One choice that was going to have a big impact on my life at this time was—ta da—my college major. It needed to fit my skills and personality and passions. It needed to feel right, and it needed it to *be* right. I had a family to support. I needed a grownup job. I hoped it would serve me for the rest of my life.

Heavy responsibilities weighed on me. I needed to get going with my life, to start moving forward with a firm commitment to a career path. But in what direction?

Isn't it interesting when you're at a crossroads and under a lot of stress when a new path opens up to you?

While I was struggling with making a decision about my major, somehow a clear vision of a method that would help me decide opened up to me. It just came into my heart. It was so simple that it seemed too obvious for me to have not seen it before. I didn't know what to call it then, but now I call it the *reflection method.*

The reflection method worked for me like nothing I'd ever tried before. I used it to choose my college major (English is what it turned out to be), and, looking back, it was one of the best decisions I have ever made in my career and life. It became the foundation of a successful and happy writing career, a career I've never tired of or gotten bored with.

I wrote this little book to share with you the decision-making process I discovered. It's a step-by-step program, simple and effective. I've been using it for many years, and now, finally, I have put it down in black-and-white so I can easily share it with others, including you.

Note: The reflection method works well for non-binary decisions, that is, decisions with three or more options, not merely a choice between yes or no. If you are faced with a binary decision, replace top ten, top five, and top three lists (you'll see them later in the book) with your top-ten, top-five, or top-three pro-con lists.

While I first used this process to choose what to study in college, I've used this system for making many kinds of decisions. It is especially effective when you have many options open to you, which is the case for many of us in our complex world—we have incredible opportunities open to us and it's difficult to sort through all the options when you feel like you're stuck in a pinball machine.

This little volume will help you to get focused, a key to decision making. The approach will help you uncover unconscious feelings, that self-incarceration that holds us back from doing things without us really knowing why.

What's behind those feelings that hold you back?

The War inside Your Brain

Your brain is divided into two hemispheres. They are connected by millions of axonal fibers, but those hemispheres are separate. It can make it feel like you're two people in one.

Your right brain is visionary and sees things in pictures, not in words. Your left brain sees things as orderly sequences, in boxes large and small, and in language. Your right brain sees the big picture, the big now; your left brain wants to be logical because it sees the past and thinks it can predict the future.

Sometimes the different sides of your brain get into a fight. That may be why you feel so restless when making a big decision! Your right brain is intuitive, but doesn't express itself in words; your left brain argues its logical points with language. When the sides don't see "neuron to neuron," you feel unsettled, agitated, and at times even angry. That pit in your stomach comes in large part from a hemispheric détente.

The process in this book uses both sides of your brain. I didn't know this at the time I discovered the system, but it is clear to me now what happened: I found a way to quiet my mind by listening to both sides of my brain fair and square.

In this book, you'll use logic and language to create lists that will satisfy your left brain, and then you'll use meditation to allow your right brain to envision your big picture. The result is that both sides of your brain will be completely happy with you. The fight will be over. At least that's been true for me.

The Seven Steps

Now, let's look at how this book is organized. It's broken down into seven reflective steps:

- Step 1: Brainstorming
- Step 2: Your Top Ten
- Step 3: Your Top Five
- Step 4: Your Top Three
- Step 5: Your Number One
- Step 6: Take Time to Process
- Step 7: Make a Great Decision

As a running example, I'll use the process of choosing a career. Yep. I won't address all the possible issues surrounding this decision, but I'll touch on some of the most important ones, which will be evident as you walk through the steps.

Though I'll use career choice as an example, you should insert your own decision here. Before taking the first step, write down on a separate piece of paper or in a computer file what you want to make your decision about. If you have a paperback version of this book, you can write your statement and other lists in the space provided.

Note: If you're trying to make a decision *for* another person without their knowledge or consent, that decision is destined to fail, no matter if you use this system or any other system. Unless you're partnering on a decision and you have the other party's full consent, make decisions for yourself only.

WHAT IS YOUR DECISION ABOUT?

The pre-step is to write down what your decision is about.

1

BRAINSTORMING YOUR LIST

THE FIRST STEP is one you're likely familiar with: Brainstorming. Yep, the mind dump, a right brain activity. You'll be looking for raw materials. It's like mining your subconscious and you'll leave tailings behind as you search for gems.

This can be scary. Sometimes you want to hide from your subconscious mind. You don't want to face what's way down in the mine shaft. These fears act like thieves hiding in the dark corners of your thoughts. They don't have your best interests at heart.

As long as they're hidden, they may be stealing from you. Your job is to chase them out from their hiding places, confront them, make them pay for their mischief, and, if necessary, take them into custody. Arresting these criminals of the mind means you ID them and put them on paper. Then you're on the way to being in control of these sneaky little cheaters of your future.

The Catalyst

A trick to use here is to find a tool that will help trigger your thought processes. The tool I used when I discovered this system was a paperback college catalog. It was my catalyst for coming up with a list of college majors, and it worked like a charm.

Probably the best tool you could use right now if you're making a decision about a career (following the example in this book) is to use an Internet-based catalog or anything similar. You could use that as the catalyst for your choices as I used a college catalog for mine. Use any resource you like to trigger your mind—online listings, magazines, books, reference sets—anything that will trigger free flowing ideas in the area you're making a decision about.

As you start searching for ideas, write anything that comes to mind, whether in the form of pictures or in words—anything! This is a freeing exercise because it gives both your right and left brains permission to express themselves. Write your ideas in the space provided at the end of this chapter if you have the paperback; if not, write them on a separate piece of paper or in a computer file or in a note-taking app on your smart phone.

For example, if you were using the career case, grab your resource and start thumbing or scrolling through it. Remember, if your source is vast, your right brain loves vast. Things will jump off the page at you. Write them all down. Write furiously. Pay attention to everything. Be thorough. Be honest with yourself. Give any shiny thing in the grass a chance.

Finally, a word about weighting your score. You can (and should) give each item on the list a weight or a level of importance to you. Use a scale of 1 through 5, or 1 through 10, or 1 through 100, whichever you prefer.

Where does this weight come from? It comes from your own inner *importometer*. (Yes, I made that word up.) Your impor-tometer comes from your right brain, the part that expresses itself with feelings, "Oh, wow, I really like that!" Or "That's okay. Good enough." Or "Forget about it."

What you're looking for is an immediate, gut reaction. When you feel a non-verbal impulse, it's coming from your right brain. After you acknowledge that impulse and write it down, you can let your left brain give it a weight, in the form of a number.

Write down your brainstorming list, including a weight for each item listed. It is important that you don't edit your choices right now. Let them flow. Let everything fly out and land on paper (or in a file). Comfort your left brain by reminding it that careful editing will come later. Write down whatever pops up, even if it only slightly intrigues you.

Most of all, have fun with this part!

Note: If you're making a binary, yes-or-no decision, you can use this time or space to focus on your why-and-why-nots, your initial, gut impressions, your pros and cons. Don't worry about organization at this point—that will come later. Just let your thoughts present themselves to your conscious mind, whether positive or negative, and then write them down.

BRAINSTORMING LIST

Jot down or type your ideas, then assign them each a numbered weight of importance.

2

YOUR TOP TEN

Now that you have finished your brainstorming session and have written down your list of careers (or whatever decision you chose to focus on), go back to the list and highlight the ones that really stand out for you. Use a highlighter or the highlight feature for your application.

Which ones really excited you and got you pumped up? Which ones matched your passions in life? Your goal here is to highlight at least 10 items on your brainstorm list.

Next, you'll prioritize a list of ten items. Do this by numbering the items on your brainstorming list, to the left of the item.

Again, follow your intuition or gut feeling. This is a right brain free for all. Don't mull, judge, condemn, or agonize. That's your left brain trying to rain on your parade. Just go with your intuition—let your right brain "speak." Prioritize first and ask questions later.

Remember, your right brain likes to choose based on feelings; your left brain likes to logically organize things.

Do this as quickly as you can. You may have highlighted more than ten items. If so, drop any items numbered 11 or greater. That's where you make the cut.

Now, set the list aside for a time, perhaps 30 to 60 minutes, but maybe several hours, or even a day or two. You choose the amount of time you take, not me. It's up to you. The important point is that you come back to the list fresh after a clean break.

After you come back to the list, number your top ten one more time. You may have a different sequence than your first run through. That's good! When you're done, renumber them or write them down or type them in the new order (if you've prioritized them differently) in the space provided in the paperback or separately if you don't have that.

As you list your top ten items in order, give each item a weight. The greater the number, the more weight or importance it has to you. Again, use a scale of 1 through 5, 1 through 10, or whatever works for you. The weight of the item should influence its order. Play with your lists and be open to late changes.

Note: If you're making a binary decision (yes or no), try instead to create ten pro and ten con points to weigh and consider. It's best to weight each point, such as on a scale of 1 through 10, to help you discern which points are the most important to you. Use these weights to order your pros and cons.

TOP TEN LIST

List your top ten, then prioritize them and give them each a weight.

1. _____
2. _____
3. _____
4. _____
5. _____
6. _____
7. _____
8. _____
9. _____
10. _____

3

YOUR TOP FIVE

OKAY, now that you have taken a break, it's time to pare down your top ten list and turn it into a top five.

Go back to your list of ten items. Using your intuition-gut, number the list of ten again. That's right, order them a third time.

Don't listen to that neural noise—go with your right-brainish feelings! Let them have their say.

You may come up with the same numbers for the list as you did the last time, or it may be surprisingly different. Pay attention to the weight you gave each item. This may be at variance with the numbered ordering. The weight is there to help correct or monitor that.

Set the list aside and ruminate again. Come back to the list after you've had enough time away from it and pick your top five. Write down your top five with weights for each.

Once more, after you've taken your first shot at your top five, take yet another breather. Set the list of five aside until you can come at it fresh. Set it aside for at least 20 minutes, but this time, no longer than one day.

Note: If you're making a binary decision (yes or no), like you did with the top ten list, try creating five pro and five con points. Also, weigh each point, such as on a scale of 1 to 10, to help you see which points are the most meaningful. Your weights can help you order your lists as well.

TOP FIVE LIST

List your top five, prioritize them, and give them each a weight.

1. _____
2. _____
3. _____
4. _____
5. _____

4

YOUR TOP THREE

Hey, you're getting closer! Using the same method you did for the top ten and top five lists, create a top three list.

I'm not trying to drive you crazy with all these lists. This is an important part of the process. The lists help you distinguish what's important to you and what's not. Trust the process and it will serve you well.

Make sure you've taken a decent break from the top five list, but no more than a day. Your brain needs time to simmer on what you have selected, but not too much time.

Somehow, it is during this in-between time—the gap—that makes a difference. Perhaps you've noticed this phenomena when you've practiced a musical instrument, or a dance step, or a sport: It is not during practice that you improve, but it's during the in-between time. For some reason, when your brain and body have the chance to go quiet, it processes, synthesizes, and adapts to new information.

You know the drill by now. Go back to the top five list and number your new list 1, 2, 3. Left brain, have at it.

Take a break. Meditate. Breathe. Think about it, but don't spend your energy debating it internally. Step into the natural flow of the ideas and go by feel. Right brain, give me wings.

Then rearrange the list again, and number it one more time, including weights, using your neglected genius. Write them down one last time.

Note: If you're making a binary decision (yes or no), as you did with previous lists, create here three pro and three con points. Give a weight to each point, on a scale of 1 to 10, for example, to help you understand which points are most valuable to you. Use your weights to order or reorder your list.

TOP THREE LIST

List your top three, prioritize them, and give them each a weight.

1. _____
2. _____
3. _____

5

NUMBER ONE

AFTER ANOTHER BREAK, come back to your top three list, and using your inspiration, circle or pick your number 1 choice.

Take another breather, and choose your number 1 one more time. Is it still the same choice? If it's different from your first choice, take another break and after that, choose your top choice one more time. Make sure you wind up choosing number 1 at least twice.

If you have followed the process, this will come easily to you. You'll feel very settled. You won't have any doubts or confusion about the choice. You may *see* it. It might feel like a view from a mountain top.

If you don't feel quite right yet, just relax and listen a little longer.

Once you feel clear and peaceful, write down or type your number one choice (no weight needed).

Note: For those making a binary, yes-no decision, this is where you weigh your pros and cons, logically, emotionally, and spiritually, and decide whether its best for you to proceed or not.

YOUR NUMBER ONE

Congratulations! You're ready to write down your number 1 choice.

6

TAKE TIME TO PROCESS

It's time to be still, an essential part of the reflection method.

Now that you've made a decision about what your number 1 choice is, give it some time. Think, meditate, and pray.

If you don't know how to pray, or who to pray to, that's okay: Just ask for what you want. Saying it out loud is best. If you have had a rest, and you still feel at peace about your top choice, you're in a good place.

Take Action

Now begin to act on your choice. If you have made a right choice, doubts will flee, your confidence will grow stronger and stronger as time passes, and you'll feel completely at peace about what you intend to do.

If you have not chosen well, you will feel like you're being tossed about in a dinghy in a storm at sea. Doubts will crowd in and the space around you will feel like it's decorated with black crepe paper. Not good. Time to think again.

If this happens to you—a dark feeling after all your hard work—your subconscious it trying to tell you something. You might at this point start the process over again with a list of ten, five, or three, or even go back to the very beginning. If you feel compelled to do this, don't worry. The investment will be totally worth it! You'll be rewarded for your patience for patience is the path to glory.

A Right Choice

Notice that I said *a* right choice, not *the* right choice. Nothing eats up your energy and *joie de vivre* like worrying about making that one and only right choice. So many choices will work out; *a* right choice is simply good enough!

We advised our children that there is no one and only person to marry until *after* you're married! Then that person becomes your one and only. Choose well, then make it right. Commit yourself to do your very best to go with your decision, to trust it, to believe in it.

The key is to be able to see a clear path in front of you. When you see your way clear, it is a sign that you have found a path worth following!

Now on to your final step.

7
___

YOUR DECISION

You've done the work. A lot of it. You've weighed your options, and you have settled on one star, one hope.

You started out with random elements from the universe of your brain and collected them into a long list. Then you chose ten items off that long list of elements.

Next, you got down to five items from the list of ten, then three from five. Finally, you picked your number 1 choice.

You've sifted through the debris of your mind, giving your left and right brains equal voice. You organized, prioritized, and reprioritized. If you're at peace, the sides of your brain are at peace too. No more *détente*.

You should feel calm and secure now. You've made a solid decision, whether you fully recognize it or not. Time for cake and ice cream. Time to congratulate yourself!

Frosting on the cake: Write down your decision in the form of a single sentence to anchor it in your heart. Write it more than once to make sure you like the wording.

YOUR DECISION AS A SENTENCE

Write down or type your decision in a single sentence. Rewrite it as often as you feel necessary, until it's as smooth as glass.

8

CONCLUDING THOUGHTS

I HOPE you've gotten out of the reflection method as much as you've put into it. I know it's deceptively simple but it's also very effective. It's been a great blessing to me, and has guided me as I've made life decisions. Every time I've used this method with discipline, I've never regretted my decisions, even many years later.

That's the key: Making a decision that you feel no need to alter or regret, one you'll feel peaceful about years down the road.

Not much can stand in the way of your making good decisions now, except you.

Never forget that you're a sovereign soul. You have the right to choose, no matter what forces come against you. Your parents may try to persuade you to their way of seeing the world. Your friends will weigh in with their own opinions. Your spouse may question your sanity, and a responsibility to children will strongly influence your direction in life.

Nevertheless, when all is said and done, *you* get to choose. Don't abdicate that right. You can't control everything, but at least you can choose what you choose for yourself.

Through this process, I hope you've been fair with yourself. I trust you've followed the steps honestly, and you've listened to the contrasting sides of your brain. Move forward now with confidence and you'll never become a member of the woulda-coulda-shoulda club!

All the best and may you be greatly blessed in life and in all your decisions.

ABOUT THE AUTHOR

Michael James Fitzgerald loves to write, read, and run. He doesn't own a television —he prefers doing something more creative with his time. He is the author of over 20 books that have been published worldwide with translations in Spanish, Portuguese, French, German, Polish, Korean, Japanese, and Chinese. You can find more about him at MichaelJamesFitzgerald.com.

ALSO BY MICHAEL JAMES FITZGERALD

As a Man Thinketh Workbook Edition (Editor)

The Science of Getting Rich Workbook Edition (Editor)

Write Your Book in 24 Hours!

www.ingramcontent.com/pod-product-compliance
Lightning Source LLC
Chambersburg PA
CBHW071747020426

42331CB00008B/2213

9 781887 309271